THEODORE

CITY KID

GINGER NIELSON

THEODORE

CITY KID

Contact: gingernielson@gmail.com
ISBN-13:978-057874028-7

Carrot Flower Books ~ 2021

~ FOR BILL ~

Theodore lived in a city of bricks, stone, and concrete.

It was a place where no one seemed to smile.

People were sad.
Cats were sad.
Dogs were sad.

Even the rats seemed sad.

One day, as Theodore walked home from school, something unexpected happened.

Cautiously, Theodore knocked on the door of the nearby building.

"May I help you?" said a woman with a sweet voice and a smile to match.

Theodore held out the flower.

"Hello, my name is Theodore.
I found this flower. It fell from
your roof. Are there plants
growing up there?"

"Why yes, there are!"
she answered. "Would you
like to see the garden?"
"Oh, yes," said Theodore.

"Mrs. Gordon lives upstairs," the lady said. "You may go up to see her if you like."

Theodore climbed the long flight of stairs. At the top he stopped to peek through the window of a brightly painted door. He opened it slowly.

Theodore stepped out onto
the roof. A woman in a floppy hat
was watering some plants.
"Hello?" Theodore said softly.
"Are you Mrs. Gordon?"

The woman turned to Theodore,
took off her gloves, and welcomed
her visitor.

"Why, yes, I am. And who might you be?"
"My name is Theodore," he said
excitedly," and I came to see your garden."

"Well, let me show you around," she said.
For almost an hour, Mrs. Gordon showed
Theodore all over the roof-top garden.
Then she asked, "Would you like some
seeds to plant on your roof?"

"I would love to have a garden too," Theodore explained, "but I have no roof for planting."

"Hmmm," Mrs. Gordon took off her hat and scratched her head.

"Maybe, I can find you a place for a garden of your own."

"Come back tomorrow after school, and we can take a look."

The next day, Theodore could hardly
wait for school to end. Mrs. Gordon was
waiting for him as she promised.
"Come on, let's go," said Mrs. Gordon.

Off they went. They walked past tall, brick buildings and black lampposts. They walked all the way to the edge of the city.

Around the corner of the last building,
Theodore saw an empty lot. A broken fence
stood at the edge of a field of weeds.

Mrs. Gordon explained that there used to be a building here, but the city had taken it down a few years ago.

"This could be a wonderful garden, if you are willing to work hard."

The next day, Mrs. Gordon and Theodore went to the lot. They even found an old water pipe and made it work.

Mrs. Gordon gave Theodore a bucket
for carrying water. In the bucket were some
tools, seeds, and four small plants. Theodore
began to work as soon as school was out
each day.

Theodore did not care how much work he would have to do. He wanted to grow a beautiful garden.

He came to the lot every day after school and worked very hard. During the summer, he worked even harder. His plants began to grow.

The season changed to autumn, and many plants went to sleep or seemed to be dying. Mrs. Gordon explained this was to be expected because plants need some time to rest.

"Next season they will be stronger," she said.

Winter came, and Theodore still visited the garden looking for signs that his garden was not gone.

Springtime arrived. Sweet fragrances drifted into the city. People noticed!

They all started coming to Theodore's garden. The garden made them happy.

Theodore offered plants to anyone who wanted them. Rainbows of color flooded the city.

One day a very special person came to see Theodore's garden.

CERTIFICATE
of
MERIT

Theodore's Garden

Your city says Thank you

The Mayor of the city was so impressed that she gave Theodore the *Key to the City* and an official *Certificate of Merit*.

The Mayor smiled as she said, "You have done so much to make all the people happy. Our city is filled with glorious color and smiling faces. Is there something we could do for you?"

Theodore smiled. Yes, there was something.

Theodore's garden was official!